A Tale of Dogged Determination

"While telling the heartwarming story of Basil, a gentle, mixed-breed rescue dog, Ms. Vandiver teaches young readers about the shelter and rescue system, caring for a dog, and the value of a loving, forever home. *Basil's Quest* also encourages kindness, compassion, and the appreciation of dogs of all breeds, sizes, and colors. While this book is intended for young folks, it is a delightful read for the entire family."

- Zina Goodin, *Co-founder,*
Old Friends Senior Dog Sanctuary, Mt. Juliet, TN

"*Basil's Quest* is a touching story of a dog desperately wanting a forever home. He endures bullying, rejection, and adapting to unfamiliar situations with courage and heart. *Basil's Quest* offers rich opportunities for discussion and understanding. The book will be enjoyed by all readers, but especially those with a love of animals."

- Martha Geel, *Retired 3rd & 4th Grade Teacher,*
Ridgeway Elementary, Columbia, MO

"This book will surely help young readers to understand the importance of love, care, and responsibility for animals in our lives by giving a glimpse into their hearts and minds."

- Vickie Harris, *Director,*
Music City Animal Rescue, Nashville, TN

"I thoroughly enjoyed reading Basil's story and was rooting for him with the turn of every page. I appreciate the work the author did to ensure the rescue story was accurately portrayed. You, too, will fall in love with Basil."

- **Elizabeth Chauncey,** *Founder and President, East C.A.N.,*
East Nashville, TN

"*Basil's Quest* is a compelling story told from a pup's perspective about compassion, patience, and healing. Basil shows us how to forgive and love again, especially when bullying is discussed. It serves as a friendly reminder that bullying is hurtful to everyone, not just children. It's a story with uplifting highs, lonely lows, and a happy ending. Highly recommended."

- **Tara Rose,** *Guest Educator,*
Enriched Schools, Nashville, TN

"*Basil's Quest* is a beautiful story and a delight to read. From the opening lines of the book, I was drawn into Basil's world and his search for a forever home. He meets many people on his path, some loving and some indifferent, but through it all he trusts that he will end up where he is supposed to be. I found myself identifying with Basil and his journey because isn't a safe, cozy home, and good people in our lives what we all want?"

- **Susan Kelley,** *Founder,*
Bow Wow Film Festival

BASIL'S QUEST

A Tale of Dogged Determination

BASIL'S QUEST
A Tale of Dogged Determination

Gracie H. Vandiver

Illustrations by
Amanda Penecale

11/22 Publishing
Nashville, TN

11/22 Publishing
P.O. Box 60863
Nashville, TN 37206-0863

Library of Congress Control Number: 2021909118 (hardcover)

ISBN 978-0-9717745-2-0 (hardcover)
ISBN 978-0-9717745-3-7 (paperback)
ISBN 978-0-9717745-4-4 (eBook)

Author's photo by Brandon Jackson
Lyrics from Chillout © 2008 by Ze Frank
were used with permission.

For Aurora and Asher
I hope you like Nana's story.

Dogs do speak, but only to those
who know how to listen.
- Orhan Pamuk
Recipient of the 2006 Nobel Prize in Literature

1

I often escape my yard and wander around the neighborhood, hoping that a kind person will find me and adopt me into their family. I long for a new life, a life where I won't live with mean dogs that constantly bully me and steal my food. A life where I sleep on my owner's cozy bed. A good life where I can love fully and feel loved in return. But every time I escape, my neighbors always find me and bring me back.

This time, I'm scared and shivering in the pouring rain, farther than I have ever been from my house and any house I recognize. The boisterous thunder scares me. I keep my tail tucked down tightly under my body. Sheets of water strike my face and I can barely see. I think I hear my name, but no, that's highly unlikely. After all, no one is out looking for me. I'm sure of it. No one.

I hear my name again but this time I know it's for real because when I squint through my wet and heavy eyelids, I see Jolie standing by her car. The back door is swung wide open. "Basil. Here boy! Basil! Baaaasil!" she yells.

I dash to Jolie's back seat and jump in.

"Oh, Basil. You're so far from home! You poor baby! Oh my gosh. You're drenched!"

I shake every inch of my body from head to tail. My black hair splatters water all over Jolie's car. Oops!

"Oh, sweetheart. You poor thing."

Jolie gets out of her car, opens the trunk, and returns with a huge fluffy beach towel. She leans into the back seat and covers me with the nice dry towel, rubbing and patting me down. Then she wipes the splatters off all the doors and windows.

"There you go, sweetie. That should make you feel better."

Jolie drives us to her house, which is just around the corner from where I live. Notice I say "where I live." I don't call it home. It's never felt like home to me. A home is where you are loved and cared for.

We park in her driveway. She keeps the engine

running with the heater on full blast aimed in my direction. Taking her cell phone from her purse, Jolie calls my owner. The fierce rain pounds the roof of the car.

She shouts, "Trish? This is Jolie . . . JOLIE! I've got Basil in my car. I was driving home and I spotted him six blocks away this time. He's lucky he didn't get hit by a car in this storm."

Jolie listens for what feels like a long time. I'm really good at reading body language. The look on her face says this conversation isn't going well.

"The Humane Association doesn't come get animals. They don't do that. They only take in dogs by appointment and you have to bring them there."

Another long pause.

"Well, if you've been thinking of finding Basil a new home, would you be willing to surrender him to me? I'll find someone to foster him and I'll work on finding him a permanent home."

This time, a shorter pause.

"Okay, Trish. Yes, I do understand. Sometimes dogs just don't get along. I'm sorry it's caused so much stress since you moved back home with Victor. Thank you for letting me help. You know I only want the best for Basil. I promise I'll find him a good home."

Jolie hangs up and turns to me. "Basil, you're such an awesome dog. If we didn't already have two dogs, I would keep you myself."

Jolie makes another call. "Hello, Hannah? Hey, it's Jolie. Listen, I hate to ask this, but I really need a favor. I found my neighbor's dog when I was driving home from work just now. I've found him at least a half-dozen times over the past two years and always brought him home. But this time his owner said she was going to tie him to a tree because she's tired of him escaping, and she'd bring him to the Humane Association in the morning. I couldn't bear the thought of him being tied up outside, especially without shelter. You know how these spring storms can easily turn into tornadoes, so I persuaded her to surrender the dog to me. Now I need to find someone to foster him. I know I'm asking a lot, but would you be willing to take him in, even if it's just for the night? I would be so incredibly grateful."

This time, a very short pause.

"Well, I'm not really sure what he is. Maybe a black Lab? He's super sweet. Can I bring him by so you can meet him?" Jolie sounds quite desperate and convincing.

"Thank you, Hannah! You're the best. I'll be there in twenty."

With a big smile on her face, Jolie says, "Basil, I'm so excited. Hannah loves dogs so much that she owns a doggie day care center. She's staying late just so she can meet you!"

Jolie drives through rainy East Nashville streets while giving me the scoop about Hannah and Hannah's Haven, her doggie day care center. Jolie recently got a part-time job there. How lucky those dogs must be to get to spend so much time with Jolie.

Whoa! The crack of more thunder startles me. I lower my head. My ears tuck back to block the noise. Jolie sees my reaction in her rearview mirror and starts singing a little tune: "Hey. You're okay. You'll be fine. Just breathe." Jolie keeps her left hand on the steering wheel and reaches into the back seat to rub my ear. She sings this song over and over and my anxiety melts away.

2

I remember the first time I met Jolie. It was an early crisp spring morning two years ago. I remember it well because it was my first adventure when I was finally brave enough to sneak out of my yard. You see, part of the wooden fence on the far side of the yard had rotted-out planks at the bottom. I discovered there was just enough room for me to squeeze out. It was my secret passage.

I walked a whole block, taking my time to enjoy all the heavenly new scents of flowers and grass, and came upon Jolie watering her roses in her front yard. Her dogs wagged their tails at me from behind the driveway gate.

Jolie looked up from her roses. "Hey, buddy. Where'd you come from? I've never seen you before.

Hmm. You look a little thin. Are you hungry? Yeah, I thought so. Wait right there." I loved how gentle she was, so I did as I was told.

She turned off the hose and went inside her house. She came back out carrying a pie tin of kibble and put it on the ground in front of me. Jolie took a few steps back. In a soft, reassuring voice, she said, "It's okay. It's for you."

I'd never taken food from a stranger before, but that didn't stop me from scarfing it down!

"So, how are we going to figure out where you live if you don't have a tag on your collar?"

Jolie's friend, Celine, walked toward us. "Hey, Celine! Why are you walking down the street with a leash in your hand and no dog?"

"I just dropped off Tink at my mom's house for a play date with her dog. I meant to leave the leash, but I walked out with it in my hand and I didn't feel like walking back. Hey, who's this?"

"I don't know but he's friendly. How would you like to take him home and I'll work on finding his owner? It's only fair. I have two dogs and you only have one."

"I know it's my turn to foster, but Sam and I are leaving on vacation this weekend."

"I definitely can't take him because my dogs will

go crazy if I bring another dog into the house. If you can't help, then I'll bring him to Metro Animal Care and Control and cross my fingers that his owners will reach out to MACC to find him. They'll take great care of him, but it's a scary place for a stray with all the barking and cages."

"Well, I suppose I can take him today, but if we don't find his owner by the time we leave, I'll need to hand him off to you."

"That will at least buy us a couple of days to find his owner. I'll reach out on social media and I'll also call MACC to let them know we found a stray, just in case someone calls and describes him. In fact, I think they have a form that can be filled out online for that."

They joked about how they always tag-teamed whenever they found a stray. Celine said, "I'll take him to the vet to have them scan for a microchip. That sure makes finding owners easier. Besides, if we need to bring him to the animal shelter, their first priority is always to reunite animals with their owner if there's a chip with the contact info. I'll let you know what I find out."

Celine hooked the leash to my collar, and I walked with her up the alley. We reached the back-yard leading to her house and climbed the steps to a big wooden deck. She opened her back door and I gladly followed her inside.

My nose got excited from all the new scents.

Celine fluffed up a large round dog bed perched in the corner of the kitchen. She patted the bed a couple of times while she looked at me. "Here you go. Tink won't mind if you use her bed."

Celine called Sam and left a message on his voicemail. "Hey, it's me. Just a head's up. Jolie found a loose dog with a collar and no tag. We're fostering him until we leave for vacation. Hopefully, it won't take long to find his owner. Okay. Love you. See you soon!"

She put her phone down on the kitchen table and started preparing dinner. Boy, did her kitchen smell delicious! Like food that humans eat.

The porch screen opened and clicked shut and Sam, a tall thin man, walked in. "Hi, sweetheart. I got your message when I was a couple blocks away." Sam knelt down and stroked my back. "I think I've seen this dog before over on Porter Road. You know, the house with the white picket fence? Let's walk him over there."

Celine turned off the stove. Sam clicked Tink's leash to my collar, and they walked me back to

Victor's house. After a lot of persistent and loud knocking, Victor finally answered the door.

When Sam asked if I was his dog, he brusquely answered, "He's my daughter's dog. Put him in the yard."

Then, without another word, Victor slammed the front door shut.

3

The lightning and thunder jar me out of my memories as Jolie pulls into a parking space in front of a large brick building. She takes her phone from her purse and sends a text. A minute later, Hannah comes out to the car holding a large white umbrella with pictures of dogs on it.

Hannah looks confused as she slowly studies me through the car window. It's only open a few inches because of the rain.

"I don't know, Jolie. His face is kind of weird looking. Could be stress."

"He's been living outside twenty-four/seven for over two years. He's probably never been in a car, so maybe what you're seeing is that he's just scared. Besides, who wouldn't be scared in this crazy storm we're having? Trust me. I know this dog really well and he's a sweetheart."

"Well, why don't you bring him inside and let me have a better look."

Jolie leads me out of her car to the inside of Hannah's Haven. The loud ringing from a strand of bells hanging on the inside doorknob startles me, so I step back behind Jolie. I've never seen a place quite like this. In fact, before today, I didn't even know it existed!

The front room has a wooden bench, a big potted tree-like plant, and a large metal dog bowl with fresh water. The bright overhead lights and sunny yellow walls are sure a stark contrast to the rainy gray sky outside!

Hannah crouches down, avoiding eye contact with me. I walk up to her to get a good whiff. She smells like so many different kinds of dogs, but mostly of poodle.

"Hannah, I know I'm asking a lot, but if you'll foster him, I promise I'll do everything I can to find him a good home. You have my word."

Hannah sighs. "It's gonna take some work since it's always harder to place a black dog in a home. For some reason, people are just more attracted to other colors. That's why shelters usually have more black dogs than anything else. Since my last foster was just adopted, I guess it won't be too much trouble to take him in, but on two conditions: We're all out of kibble and I don't believe in feeding fosters any less quality of food than I feed my own dogs. So how about if I write a check and you go to the pet store down the street to get him kibble before they close? Then, when you get back, you can give him a much-needed bath."

"Thank you, Hannah! You won't be sorry."

After Jolie leaves, Hannah crouches down in front of me, and in the softest voice she assures me, "It's okay, Basil. You're safe now. We won't let anything bad happen to you."

I hang out with Hannah in her office. Hannah sits behind a big wooden desk. I look up at her munching on chocolate-covered almonds. She drops one on the floor and I go for it.

"Sorry, Basil. Chocolate isn't good for dogs. But here, I have a dog biscuit you might like."

She returns to her laptop, scrolling through pictures she's taken of clients' dogs as she twirls her curly blond hair around her finger.

She notices me staring up at her. "Feel free to explore, Basil. There's nothing you can't touch in my office."

I do love to explore. The large plastic dog crate in

the front corner of the room grabs my attention. There's a big white poodle inside. I was right! I did catch the scent of poodle on Hannah. The poodle doesn't seem at all concerned that I'm here.

"That's my dog, Chelsea. You don't have to worry about her. She's quite happy just hanging out in her crate while I work."

Next, an area directly across the room from Hannah's desk arouses my interest. I start sniffing a large round shaggy rug.

Hannah looks up. "That's where my daughter, Ivy, plays when she comes to work with me. It's fine to sniff but don't chew anything, okay?"

Got it, Hannah. There's a futon against the wall with bright pink and purple pillows decorating it and a variety of stuffed animals all neatly lined up against the pillows. I spend a long time taking in the smells that linger from when Ivy was there last.

After I have my fill of scents, I lay on the floor by Hannah's desk and wait for Jolie to return. I picture Jolie singing the Chillout song to me. "Hey. You're okay. You'll be fine. Just breathe."

4

A woman reeking of perfume pops into Hannah's office. A dachshund sticks out of her large canvas shoulder bag.

"Well now, who do we have here? Isn't he a cutie? Hey there, sweetie!" She takes a giant step back. "Ooh. What's that smell?"

"Hi, Leigh Ann. That smell is Basil. Jolie's neighbor surrendered him to her, and I agreed to foster him while we try and find him a new home. I didn't have the heart to turn him away, even if he is a little odd looking."

Now I'm confused. Wasn't I just called a cutie?

Leigh Ann takes the dachshund out of the shoulder bag and puts him on the floor.

"Mr. Basil, meet Dooley. Dooley, this is Basil.

He's going to be staying with us tonight so let's make him feel welcome."

I like her happy disposition. And Dooley seems pretty chill.

The bells on the front door start jingling, and Jolie's back with a large bag of kibble.

"Hey there, Leigh Ann. I see you've met Basil. Want to help me give him a bath?"

Leigh Ann walks down a long hallway toward a different part of the building. "Sure. C'mon, Dooley. C'mon, Basil. Basil, we're gonna get ya all cleaned up. You're gonna smell so good. You won't even recognize yourself."

Jolie and Leigh Ann remove plastic full-length aprons from a hook on the wall and fasten them. They lift me into a ginormous metal tub. Jolie takes hold of a long rubber hose with a nozzle on the end. She turns two handles until she feels the water temperature is just right, then wets me down all over from head to tail and back again. With the other hand, she covers my ears, being careful not to get water in them. Then Leigh Ann pours shampoo across my back. She works the shampoo into lots of bubbles and reaches around to spread it on my belly, legs, and tail, while Jolie props me up with her arms under my belly so I can't sit down. They rinse and repeat the whole process to make sure they've gotten all the dirt off. It tickles!

To be honest, I do love the attention. The two of them talk to me and dote on me until all the caked-on dirt is washed down the drain and my coat is squeaky clean. Jolie wets a washcloth, wrings it out, and gently wipes my face clean.

They lift me out of the tub, cover me with a soft towel, and rub me dry.

"Okay, Leigh Ann. I'm leaving my buddy here in your care. Basil, sleep tight and I'll see you in the morning."

Jolie plants a kiss on my wet forehead, then heads back down the hallway to the front door.

Good night, Jolie.

5

Leigh Ann asks, "Are you hungry?" My ears perk straight up! We go to the feeding area and she opens the new bag of kibble, then stands back and stares at me. "Hmm. You look a little thin, Basil. I think I'll give you two cups of food."

When she sets the bowl down in front of me, Dooley just acts like it's none of his business and he trots off to another room. What a cool little dude! I'm so used to scarfing down my food because Victor's mean dogs thought nothing of eating what was in their own bowls, then growling and pushing me away to eat what I didn't have a chance to finish. Every night I went to sleep feeling hungry. I spent so many nights wishing upon the brightest star that I could live anywhere else. Anywhere.

Hannah calls out from the front door, "I'm leaving, Leigh Ann. Thanks for taking care of Basil tonight. See you tomorrow."

"No problem, Hannah. See ya."

There is a special room at Hannah's Haven where Leigh Ann and other night care staff sleep. It's small and cozy.

Leigh Ann says, "Well, Mr. Basil, overnight dogs usually stay in a separate room, but since you're the only one in my care tonight, I'll let you sleep in my room."

She brings in a big fluffy dog bed and sets it down on the floor next to her bed. Leigh Ann puts on the evening news and changes into her pajamas. She brushes and flosses her teeth. Her movements are deliberate. She seems so confident, and for the first time in a long time, I feel safe.

Watching Leigh Ann getting ready for bed makes me think of Marina, the only person I've ever loved.

Before I was taken to Victor's house, he and Trish separated and were talking about getting a divorce. Trish and Marina, their ten-year-old daughter, moved out of the house and into an apartment. Because Marina was feeling so sad about her parents' breakup, Trish adopted me from the shelter and gave me as a present to Marina on Christmas morning to cheer her up. Marina and I became best friends!

Every evening, Marina took a bath before bedtime. She chose a book from her bookshelf to read to me. I curled up with my back leaning against her in bed. When story time was over, she closed the book and put it on her nightstand.

Trish would come in to give Marina a goodnight kiss. "Good night, Marina. I love you."

"Good night, Mommy. I love you. And I love you too, Basil."

Marina wrapped her arm around me as she drifted off to sleep. I love that I was able to comfort her.

I had a good life. I had a purpose. But it came to an abrupt end when Trish's landlord showed up one cold winter day reminding her that, "According to the terms of the lease, dogs are not allowed in the apartment."

Leigh Ann's voice grabs my attention. "Okay, puppers. Let's go out in the yard so y'all can relieve yourselves before we turn in for the night." I follow Dooley. He knows where he's going like he's done this a hundred times before. Probably has.

Back inside, Leigh Ann brings Dooley into bed with her. I rest my head on the edge of the bed and look up at Leigh Ann with big adoring eyes, hoping for permission to jump up.

"Dooley, should we let Basil spend the night on the bed with us?"

I can hardly believe my good luck. I haven't slept on a bed since I lived with Marina, and that was over two years ago. I feel sad when I think of her because I miss her so much. Luckily, dogs are pretty good at adapting to new situations. I jump onto the foot of the bed and curl up so as not to take up too much space.

Good night, Dooley! Good night, Leigh Ann!

6

Sometimes, right when I'm about to fall asleep, I have a recurring memory:

"Victor? It's Trish. Listen, I really hate to ask this, but I need a favor. It's not actually for me, it's for Marina. My landlord won't let me keep Basil, and Marina will be so heartbroken if we have to give him up. She's gotten so attached to him. Would you please take Basil? Then at least he'll be at the house when Marina visits on weekends."

Trish waits for his reply.

"Yes, I know I should have checked with my landlord before getting a dog, but I didn't, and now I'm asking you for help."

Trish is silent again and she looks like she's about to cry.

"Yes, Victor, I know you already have two dogs, but Basil is really easy, and he won't be much trouble at all, and I'm sure he'll get along well with Ninja and Jet."

She pulls the phone away from her ear. I hear Victor yelling. His voice scares me. I automatically tuck my ears back, closer to my head.

"Victor, I'm not asking you to do this for me. It's for Marina. You know how much she loves Basil. When she plays with him, she forgets how sad she is and how guilty she feels about our separation."

I don't hear Victor's reply, but Trish says a bit impatiently, "I don't know why she feels guilty. Maybe she thinks the separation was her fault. Look, if you won't take him, then I'll have to bring him back to the shelter. Marina will never see him again and she'll never forgive me. Please, Victor! Please don't break Marina's heart!"

Trish muffles the phone as she softly sobs. I want to comfort her, but I'm not sure how. I move closer to Trish and she rests a hand on my back.

"Yes, I understand you're busy. I appreciate that, but if I can't bring Basil over now, I'll get evicted. Please. It won't take long. I can be there in fifteen minutes."

Trish drives me to Victor's house. It's a blustery

winter day. Only the pine and cedar trees are green. The wind whips some leaves around, but Trish keeps the car window rolled down enough so I can stick my head out. My ears flop around wildly in the wind. My nostrils are teeming with scents of damp grass from last night's rain that waft in the cold breeze.

She pulls up to Victor's, leaves the car engine running, and with my leash in hand, we quickly walk up to a big white two-story house. Two large scruffy dogs bark and come running up to the chain-link fence at the end of the driveway. They snarl loudly when they see me. I do my best to show them I'm not a threat by dropping my tail down and not looking them in the eyes. They sense my fear. I pull on my leash to get Trish to go back to the car, but that only makes her shorten the lead and pull me in closer.

Trish knocks on the big wooden front door. We wait. She glances at her watch then knocks again, this time louder. When Victor doesn't answer, we go around the side of the wrap-around porch and Trish looks through the windows. The mean dogs are rowdy as they jump up and rattle the chain-link fence. We walk back to the front and she pulls out her phone and calls Victor but hangs up when he doesn't answer. Trish mutters something. She looks at her watch a second time. Now she pounds on the door.

Victor finally opens it. He's a large man who towers over Trish. He makes me nervous, or maybe I'm just sensing how Trish feels. The fur on my neck bristles.

Trish and Victor don't speak for very long. Neither of them wants to chitchat; their conversation is businesslike. I look up and see tears in Trish's eyes as she hands my leash to Victor. She turns away without even saying goodbye to me.

Victor pulls on my leash and takes me inside. The house smells like it hasn't had the windows open in a long time. He leads me to the rear of the house, removes my leash, and points. "Go outside. Dogs are for work, not for pets. You belong in the yard. Now go."

He slams the door shut behind me and I feel very, very sad.

7

L eigh Ann's gentle touch strokes my back. "Wake up, Basil. I think you're having a bad dream. It's okay, pup."

I let out a sigh of relief. I jump off the bed and give my body a good shake. It helps me return to this moment.

Leigh Ann puts on her bathrobe and slippers, and we all trudge outside.

Nashville can get pretty hot and humid, and dogs need to stay out of the sun. It's early morning and even though the sun's still low in the sky, I can already feel that it's going to be a very hot, sticky day.

I start at the far corner of the yard, walking along the path that's been worn next to the chain-link fence. Tantalizing dog scents linger from the day before. For a dog, taking in the scents is like reading the news. Our noses have over 100 million sensory receptors! When I take in another dog's scent, I find out what they like to eat and what kind of mood they're in. Plus, dogs can sniff in stereo. One of my nostrils identifies a smell and the other nostril tells me where it's coming from. I bet humans wish they could do that.

I "go potty" (as humans like to say), then head back to Leigh Ann. Dooley comes running up to me acting like he wants to play. I'm not sure what to do. My instinct is to bow down with my front legs, then take off running around the yard. It works! Dooley and I take turns chasing each other, running around and around the whole yard until we are completely worn out.

Leigh Ann has a big grin on her face. "C'mon y'all," she yells as she waves her arm. "Time to eat."

Mmmm. The kibble in my bowl is so delicious and I don't have to scarf it down. I actually feel full after licking my bowl clean. What a wonderful new sensation in my belly!

It's like a genie granted me three wishes. I feel safe because I no longer live with Victor's mean scary dogs; I slept on Leigh Ann's comfy bed all night long; and those stabbing hunger pains have disappeared!

Jolie walks through the front door, flipping on the ceiling lights to brighten things up for the new dogs arriving for check-in. I run up to greet her.

"Basil, my love! Did you have a good night?" she asks while squatting down and rubbing my back. "How did he do, Leigh Ann?"

"He was great. Don't tell Hannah but I confess that I let him sleep on the bed with me and Dooley. I just didn't have the heart to put him in a room all by himself. I think Dooley senses that Basil needs a little extra lovin', so he was willin' to share the bed. It was so cute. Dooley curled right up against him. I took a picture with my phone. See?"

Jolie smiles. "Awww, that's so sweet."

Hannah arrives with the big white poodle. "So, Leigh Ann, how did Basil do last night?"

"Oh, Hannah. He's such a sweetie. I'm so glad you're fostering him."

"I brought Chelsea to work with me so I can test his temperament today. Did he get a good night's sleep?"

"Most definitely."

Jolie stands behind Hannah and winks at Leigh Ann.

"Great. Let's see how he checks out."

Hannah takes Chelsea and me down the hall to the

inside yard. Hannah stands back and watches how I respond to Chelsea.

Chelsea is beautiful and self-confident. She's what they call an alpha female, the type that likes to be in charge. I admire her confidence. I let her sniff me first and then I sniff her. Hannah watches patiently. I bow to Chelsea to let her know I want to play. Chelsea doesn't want to play. Okay. Maybe she's not an early riser like I am. At this point, Hannah calls to her and puts her back in her crate in the office.

Hannah returns and stands leaning over me. I immediately sense that I'm being put through a test, so I hold still. I trust that Hannah knows what she's doing, and I don't feel afraid or challenged like a lot of dogs would with someone leaning over them. She firmly grabs my front leg near the top of it. She stays in that position for a few moments. Then she surprises me by kneeling down and giving me a hug. I put my head on her shoulder. Hugs feel good!

Next, she gently moves my front legs forward, placing me from sitting into a down position. I get all excited and stand up when Hannah puts her hand in her pocket and pulls out some treats. She puts them on the ground and walks around me while I eat them. Then, as I'm eating, she steps between me and the treats. I guess she wants to see if I growl. Hey,

Hannah, I'm a lover, not a fighter! I look up at her, waiting for permission to finish claiming my reward.

"Good boy, Basil! You're going to make some lucky person an excellent companion."

As we walk back down the hall, I see Jolie and Leigh Ann peeking through the little glass window in the door that leads back to the reception area. They're both smiling.

Hannah says, "We're in luck. He has a great disposition and passed with flying colors. We shouldn't have any problem placing him in a new home. And I believe he'll do quite well in day care too."

Jolie and Leigh Ann clap and cheer. "Yay, Basil!"

8

Hannah's Haven opens at 7:00 a.m. Most dogs arrive between 7:30 and 8:30 each day. I discover that lots of dog owners don't like leaving their dogs at home alone all day while they're at work, so they bring them to doggie day care to hang out with other dogs and play and get attention.

The building is like a big warehouse. It has concrete floors, great big windows that go up almost to the ceiling, and metal fencing on stands that can be moved around to create smaller areas as the need arises.

There are two additional rooms for dogs, separate from the main area. One of the rooms is for small dogs only. The other is for dogs that need quieter surroundings away from the hustle and bustle of the main indoor yard.

On the far end, the main playground also has a large garage door that opens up to a huge outside yard. On days when the weather is hot, the garage door stays open so dogs can go back and forth as they wish.

The yard outside has a grassy area and another area that's covered in gravel. On one end is a large shaded concrete porch. On very hot days, the big fluffy dogs lounge on the cool concrete of the covered porch. And on those days, Hannah usually brings out a plastic pool and fills it up with water. It's great fun to splash around!

There's one special spot in the far end of the yard that is my happy place. It's a big pink plastic play-house shaped like a castle! When I'm worn out from playing, or if I'm simply not in the mood to play, I jump up to the flat part of the castle roof to nap in the sun. There's only room for one dog and when I'm up there, all the other dogs leave me alone.

"My happy place."

We spend the day going back and forth between the indoor playground and the yard. Sometimes all the big dogs are outside while all the little dogs stay inside. Or it could be that the little dogs are in the yard and the big dogs are inside. Or maybe one of the special groups of dogs is in the yard. Hannah makes sure that we all have lots of changes in our environment during the day so we don't get bored.

Dogs that are brought to doggie day care get way more attention and have a lot more fun than if they sleep at home the whole time their human is at work. And besides, dogs need exercise! At Hannah's, dogs get tired out during the day so when their humans pick them up, they can enjoy a more relaxing evening together. It seems to be a very popular lifestyle for dogs and their owners, and I'm grateful that I get to experience this!

9

On my second day at Hannah's Haven, Hannah chooses to use me as her demonstration dog during class that night. In front of the whole class, Hannah says, "What we are going to do is give our dogs a clear signal of what we expect, and when they show they understand, we will use a clicker and immediately provide them with a treat. We'll be giving them lots of positive reinforcement, so don't be afraid of giving too many treats!"

There are four dogs with their humans. The humans pay attention, but the dogs are all nervous because they want to sniff each other's butts and their humans won't let them.

"I'm going to use Basil here to demonstrate. I've never worked with him before so he's the perfect dog to use as an example. If I clearly communicate my expectation to him and reinforce his positive behavior, then it's just a matter of practicing with him until he consistently responds on cue. So, watch . . . Basil, sit."

I don't sit. She gently pushes my rear down while pulling up on my leash. I sit. She immediately uses her clicker which gets my attention, and she says, "Good boy!" And I get a treat! We do that over and over. On the third try, I get it perfectly.

Hannah says, "Now that I know he understands what I want from him, we'll repeat what he learned with positive reinforcement."

Sit. Click. Treat. Sit. Click. Treat. Everyone's watching me. "Good boy!"

I love being the demonstration dog. Before this, I didn't feel like Hannah and I had bonded. But now I sense her love and acceptance.

10

J olie shows up for work the next morning and Hannah greets her enthusiastically. "I used Basil as my demonstration dog last night and he was great. He's so smart! I wish you could have seen him in class. I could not have used a more perfect dog as an example. Needless to say, I'm super impressed!"

Jolie smiles. "Wow! That's so great. I told you he was awesome!" Jolie pours herself a cup of coffee and we all go into Hannah's office.

"So, Hannah, how long have you been training dogs? And how did you learn?"

"When I was twelve, my mom had cancer. When she went into the hospital for surgery, my dad brought home a poodle for me from a rescue organization. He told me that if I was going to own a dog, I needed to read books and learn how to train it. So that's what I did. My dad knew it would give me something positive to focus on while my mom was sick.

"After getting really good at training, my parents let me take in foster dogs and I trained them too. I figured it would give them an advantage for getting adopted. I saved up all my babysitting money to pay for their kibble and toys.

"I soon discovered fostering can be an expensive proposition, but the money isn't the hardest part. The hardest part is finding a good match of a forever home no matter how long it takes, because each dog is unique and so is each human.

"A dog that's been fostered has the bonus of someone getting to know them really well, so when a potential new owner comes along, the foster can tell them all about the dog's personality from firsthand experience."

Jolie and Hannah enjoy their early morning time together, talking about how dogs thrive when they're in the right environment. It gives me hope.

11

I easily settle into my new routine. After being fed each morning by the night care person, I'm the only dog allowed to hang out behind the front counter while dogs are being dropped off for the day.

On one particular day, a couple brings in an English bulldog named Hosmer. Hosmer has never been boarded before, and they're anxious about leaving him in someone else's care while they go on vacation. They quiz Hannah with questions like, "How long does it usually take dogs to adjust to boarding? Will you be sure to let him sleep in an open space since he doesn't like crates?" and "Could you please send us a picture so we can see how he's doing?"

They bring with them more than Hosmer needs: a

bed, a blanket, a big red rubber Kong, a rope to play tug-o-war with, a stuffed animal that squeaks, his kibble, and lots of treats.

How wonderful it must be to have owners who love you so much that they are worried about leaving you in someone else's care for a week.

Hannah reassures them. When they're finally ready to leave, Jolie walks them to the door and says, "Feel free to call as often as you like if you want to know how he's doing. And don't forget, you can watch the doggie-cam on our website." She holds the door open for them as they leave.

Hannah turns to Jolie and says, "I tested Hosmer's temperament last week. I think he'll do just fine, but it might be best if we start him off in his own area. It will give him some time to get used to the new surroundings."

Jolie escorts Hosmer to the interior part of the building and puts him in his own pen where he can still see the other dogs.

Leigh Ann takes over the front desk. Hannah and I head to the back. Hannah suggests putting me in with Hosmer to see how we do. Yippee! I get to be the trainer dog again. Love it!

When I enter the pen, Hosmer doesn't want to have anything to do with me. He moves to the far end and turns his head away from me, acting like I'm not even there. That's cool. I know how it feels to be here for the first time. I'm just going to hang out over here. You take your time figuring things out. If you feel like playing, just let me know. No rush.

It can get pretty loud in this place. Every new dog that enters adds to the circus. Dogs pair off and run around together. There's lots of playful barking, and it bounces off the hard floor, large windows, and high ceiling. Some dogs jump up and rattle the fence. If you're not used to it, it can feel pretty scary.

Twenty minutes pass and Hosmer turns and faces me. When he sees I'm nonthreatening, he walks toward me, wagging his tail. This is a good sign, a very good sign. Still, I don't want to spook him, so I stay put and let him approach me. Sure enough, he bows and wants to play with me. It's the coolest thing ever. I never made a friend before, but I always knew I could do it.

I look over at Hannah. She and Jolie are smiling. I hear Hannah tell Jolie, "Basil has a real talent for making new arrivals feel safe."

12

If I had to guess, I'd say that on any given weekday there are around thirty dogs at Hannah's Haven. There are usually a few dogs staying over on any given night. I've gotten pretty good at predicting which regulars show up on which days.

There's Ida Mae, a beagle. Her mom, Katrina, is an attorney, and even though Ida Mae doesn't get along with any other dogs, Katrina still drops her off on her way to the office every workday. Ida Mae's bed is put next to the couch in the corner of the den. She only gets up when an employee goes in to pet her or to take her out in the yard for a change of scenery. Katrina knows this, but she figures it's better than leaving Ida Mae alone all day at home, especially because she sometimes works late.

Remington is a mixed breed with a thick long white coat and patches of black on his back. Remington has something Hannah calls "fence aggression issues." He can't be in a pen that's connected to other pens or he'll spend the entire day running up and down the fence line while barking at the dogs on the other side. So, like I said, he goes in a special area. There are two other dogs that he plays really well with: a boxer named Bingo and a yellow Labrador retriever named Princess Buttercup. At least one of them shows up every day.

Then there's Lulubelle. She has a beautiful short red coat. She's only two — that's a teenager in dog years! — and she has non-stop energy. Lulubelle has a thing for sneaking up behind Jolie in the yard and then jumping up and nipping at her elbow. I don't like it when Jolie gets nipped by an overly excited dog who can't control itself. Hannah works with Lulubelle to correct her behavior but she's not the best student. I have no idea how Lulubelle passed her temperament test. What I do know is that dogs with major problems aren't allowed to come back.

There's Delta, a border collie. Delta is what is called a tri-pawed because she has only three legs. Her dad is a photographer for the city newspaper. He often works long hours. If he gets an assignment and can't pick up Delta before closing time, he calls Hannah, and Delta spends the night.

My very favorite dog is Ringo, a brown-and-white American pit bull terrier. He belongs to Jolie and she brings him to work with her on Fridays. I perk up when Jolie walks in with Ringo! He's gentle and kind and wouldn't hurt a flea. Well, okay, maybe a flea. I love playing with him because he never gets mean or out of control. We're pals.

13

Hannah is quick to notice I get along with everyone. She observes that I'm able to remain calm even when dogs around me are stressed out, so I often end up spending the day with the difficult dogs because it puts them at ease.

I think I developed this talent from living at Victor's house. His dogs, Jet and Ninja, were always trying to stir up trouble. They were so insecure that they bullied me to make themselves feel stronger. That's what bullies do. They try to break you down. It makes them feel superior. I learned to make myself invisible. I stayed out of their way hoping they would ignore me. When I felt afraid, like during storms, I had to act all courageous or they would use my vulnerability as the perfect opportunity to pick on me.

When Hannah pairs me up with the difficult dogs, I remind myself that you just never know what they're dealing with at home.

Maybe there's a new baby in the house and the family pet has been demoted to second place, at least in the pet's eyes. Everyone oohs and ahhs over the newborn and poor Lulubelle, for example, feels left out. Then when she arrives at doggie day care, maybe her unruly behavior helps her get some of the attention she craves.

Or maybe Delta's owner has a new girlfriend, which means he's not at home as much. Delta feels lonely so she sulks the first hour after arriving at doggie day care. And being around all the energetic dogs only makes her feel like she doesn't fit in.

If Remington is cranky and wants to be left alone, maybe it's because it thundered the night before and all the noise rattled his nerves and kept him from getting enough sleep.

Those are just some examples of why I try to never take things personally. Gosh, if I did, I would never be happy because I would always be thinking about the drama around me.

I guess we all face difficulties in life. I've had my share of challenges and am just starting to see how they may have helped define me. In a good way.

14

———

Today I'm feeling very sad. Sure, I've made lots of friends while I've been in foster care, but I'm sad because every dog who comes to Hannah's Haven, whether for a day or longer, always goes home with someone who loves them. Their owners smile when they see their pups. And there are always wagging tails. And treats. And lots of hugs.

Don't get me wrong. I'm not ungrateful that Hannah is fostering me. I just yearn for a place to call home. I go to sleep every night wishing for a happily-ever-after life. I would love to bring joy to someone special! I often wonder why, during the six weeks that Hannah's been fostering me, no one has even wanted to meet me. The more I think about being homeless, the sadder I get. I decide that if someone special isn't looking for me, I'll be proactive and see if I can find them myself!

During yard time, Leigh Ann is talking on her cell phone and not paying much attention to what's going on around her. I start digging under the fence. I'm a most excellent digger. I dig a hole that's just big enough to crawl through. I slink down low and crawl my way under the fence, coming out the other side.

"I'm a most excellent digger."

No one is out there to see my great escape, and I walk down the street in hopes of finding my next owner.

I look over my shoulder for a quick second and see my friend, Snow, a sweet white German shepherd. She follows me under the fence, even though I signal her not to. When she gets to the other side, she panics and sits down in the driveway.

I'm only halfway up the block when I hear Leigh Ann calling me. I love Leigh Ann so much. I can't just ignore her because then she would get in trouble, maybe even lose her job, and I don't want that. I turn toward the sound of her voice, stop walking, and let her catch up to me.

"Basil. Where ya goin'? You scared the livin' daylights outta me by leavin' like that. Let's get you back inside."

Snow is already inside. Leigh Ann and the other employee had to lock up to go after us. They were both pretty shaken by the whole ordeal. Leigh Ann tells Hannah later how Snow and I escaped. Hannah responds, "Yeah, I was afraid something like this would happen. Poor guy. He's been here so long. I think he needs more stimulation. I'll take him home tonight. A change of scenery should help."

15

Hannah and her husband, Colin, and their daughter, Ivy, live on many acres of land about twenty minutes from downtown Nashville. We arrive just as the sun sets. Looking out the back window of Hannah's minivan, I catch a glimpse of pink light shining through the trees along the edge of their property. The stone driveway is long and lined on each side with beautiful sugar maple trees.

The driveway ends at a garage with three big doors. Hannah pushes a button on her phone and up goes the garage door to let us in. Before we are even out of the car, Colin and Ivy quickly walk toward the car, excited to greet us. Five-year-old Ivy jumps up and down in the garage. "Yay, Basil's here!"

Colin greets Hannah with a kiss. Then he comes over to me and lets me sniff his hand.

"Hey there, Basil. Welcome to Casa de Caldwell. It's not as fancy as Hannah's Haven, but I'm sure you're going to like it here."

Handing Colin my leash, Hannah asks, "Sweetheart, would you mind putting Basil with Chelsea? And Luka would probably like him, so let's put the three of them together. I'll start dinner."

Colin and Ivy lead me into the house. It's been a long time since I've seen the inside of one. Hannah was right. I did need a change of scenery. I feel better already.

I sleep in a crate next to Chelsea. On the other side of me is Ivy's dog, Luka. Hannah has four poodles in all. Luka is the only toy poodle. The other three are standard poodles, the largest of the breed. Little Luka is the color of champagne. The others are white. Luka is the oldest of the poodles and he's deaf and blind. They must all feel really safe because none of them seems to mind me being in their home. I can't help but wonder if Hannah's dogs know how good they have it living here.

Saturday morning, right after breakfast, Colin announces, "I'll be in the garden if anyone is looking for me. It's been days since I pulled weeds and I want to stay on top of things."

Since I'm allowed to roam freely here, I follow Colin to keep him company. On the way to the vegetable crops we pass a chicken coop with six chickens. In the distance, there's a large red barn and three horses grazing in the wide-open green pasture.

Colin meticulously scans the rich brown dirt for weeds. I like watching Colin. He's focused on what he's doing.

"See this, Basil? I pull the weeds up by the roots so they can't grow back."

The warm sun beating down on my coat is comforting.

Something draws my attention to the barn, and I get up to explore. Colin notices me waiting and looking back at him for approval. It's like he read my mind when he says, "That's okay, Basil. Sniff around. There are a lot of interesting scents here, much different than the ones you're used to."

I walk past the horses, and as I do, a beautiful mare with dark chestnut brown hair looks at me. She nods her head while her thick bushy tail whisks the flies off her back. I make it to the barn, and just as my nose suspects, there's something living in there. It's a huge gray cat, startled by my appearance. She raises up her back and hisses at me like she thinks she is fierce. Okay, kitty. No need to be afraid. I get it. I'll leave you alone. I run all the way back to Colin who is still working on the weeds.

In the afternoon, Ivy's friend comes over and they have a pretend tea party out on the screened-in porch. Ivy says to me, "We need to dress you properly for tea." She wraps a fluffy scarf around my neck. It's purple and frilly, something I'm sure a poodle would wear to a tea party.

I love watching Ivy and her friend at play. They make up stories and giggle a lot, happy in their pretend world. It makes me think of Marina and I'm sad. I wonder what she's doing right this moment. There's still a big place in my heart for her.

Ivy announces, "Welcome to my tea party. Today we're having tea and crumpets." She pours me a pretend cup of tea and says, "Here's a crumpet for you, Basil."

Yum. I don't know what a crumpet is, but it sure tastes like a dog biscuit!

16

The next day the three tall poodles invite me to play a game of chase. The poodles are so athletic, able to leap high into the air. They're also quick on their feet. I have a hard time catching anyone. Still, I love that they accept me and include me in the fun.

From the back door Hannah says, "I'm going into town to pick up some groceries for dinner. Colin, will you keep an eye on things until I get back? I won't be long."

"Sure, sweetie. No problem," Colin answers.

Hannah asks Ivy, "Do you want to come with Mommy?"

"Yes. Yes. I want to go with Mommy," she chirps while jumping around the kitchen.

"Okay, my two favorite girls. See you later," says Colin. He returns to yesterday's weeding.

As Hannah navigates the long stretch of driveway back to the road, I'm distracted. I watch and wonder where the road leads. Are there other farms next to this one? Do they have horses and barn cats? What about dogs? I walk while I daydream and before I know it, I'm at the end of the driveway. I begin to follow the trail of scent from Hannah's car.

The road is a narrow two-lane highway, one lane for each direction. There aren't many cars on the road, but the ones that pass me whiz by. Their whooshing sound frightens me and the wind whips against my face. I cautiously walk on the side of the road so I won't get hit.

"I cautiously walk on the side of the road so I won't get hit."

My daydreaming ends abruptly when a car horn blares out at me. Uh-oh. Where am I? I'm lost! Oh no!

I tell myself not to panic. I take a deep breath and the Chillout song that Jolie used to sing to me comes to mind. "Hey. You're okay. You'll be fine. Just breathe."

I stop walking and start thinking things through. I was traveling the same direction as Hannah, so that means she'll come back this way and will pass me on her way home. I just need to hold still. But wait! What if she doesn't see me? What if it gets dark and I'm still standing here? As I exhale, I remind myself that negative thoughts never did anyone any good. "Hey. You're okay. You'll be fine. Just breathe."

An old truck stops by the side of the road and a man in faded overalls gets out. He approaches me with his hand out. He looks like he wants to grab my collar. "Hey, fella. I'm not gonna hurt you." He moves toward me. I feel scared and I back up. The man keeps coming toward me.

"Basil! Here, Basil!" I imagine I'm hearing Colin's voice. Then I see his big silver truck! He parks on the side of the road and runs to me, carrying a leash in his hand.

The stranger takes off hurriedly.

"Oh my gosh, Basil. You scared me so much. Now what would I have said to Hannah if you had gotten lost? Or even worse, you could have been hit by a car. C'mon, buddy. Let's go home."

I gladly jump onto the front seat of Colin's truck and he drives me back to Casa de Caldwell. Wow! That was a close one!

Later in the evening, the house fills with delicious smells. Hannah cooks a veggie nut loaf. I lay at her feet under the table and eavesdrop on their conversation while the family eats dinner.

Colin confesses, "I'm really sorry I wasn't watching Basil more closely this afternoon. I had no idea he would wander off like that. Today could have had such a horrible ending. I'm glad he's safe. He has such a gentle spirit."

Hannah responds, "I really wish you had paid more attention while we were gone. I trusted you."

"I'm so sorry, Hannah. I made a horrible mistake."

Hannah reassures him, "It could have happened to anyone, but what it tells me is that he's bored. I think he was exploring and didn't realize he left the property. Tomorrow I'm going to place an ad for him on Petfinder. I haven't been proactive enough. It's just been such a pleasure having him around. Basil has a talent for making the new dogs feel comfortable. I was ignoring his needs. Living like this isn't fair to him."

"Well, whoever adopts him better be pretty special themselves."

"Oh, don't worry. I'll make sure of that."

17

It's Monday morning and Hannah lets me hang out in her office. She types her thoughts on her computer, then calls Jolie into the office.

"What's up?" Jolie asks.

"I know you've done a really good job at getting the word out about Basil to our clientele, but since he's been here so long, I decided it's time to place an ad on Petfinder. We'll see what kind of response we get. What do you think of this?

"Breed: Labrador Retriever Mix, Sex: Male, Age: Adult, Size: Large. Loving Dog Seeks Loving Forever Home. Basil is a handsome three-year-old black Lab mix. We have introduced him to many dogs at day care. He easily adapts and plays well with all types of dogs. He's everybody's best friend. He's well-behaved and gentle with children. He is very lovable and is happiest around people. He is house-trained and crate-trained, and knows basic commands like sit, stay, down, and come. And he loves to cuddle! Please email Hannah for more information. Visit our Facebook page for more pictures and videos."

"Gosh, Hannah. I never thought I'd hear you describe Basil as handsome!"

"He *is* handsome. I think he was just really scared the day you brought him to meet me, and his facial muscles were tight or something. After he spent a few days here and realized he was safe, his expression seemed to relax. Don't worry. Someone is going to fall in love with him."

Hannah's right about me being handsome. I hope she's right about the falling in love part too.

18

Before leaving work, Jolie sits down with me. She leans in close and strokes my fur, then softly says, "Hey, buddy. I'm going on vacation and you won't see me for a week, but I promise I'll be back. I hope Hannah finds you a forever home, but part of me hopes that doesn't happen until I get back. I'd hate it if I couldn't meet your new family myself." She gives me a hug, rubs my ears, and kisses the top of my head. "I'm gonna miss you a lot, sweet pea. I'll see you in a week. Be good."

A week can feel like a long time for a dog, especially when you're separated from a human you love so deeply.

Humans have this expression, "I've got your back." I think it means they're always looking out for you. Jolie has been the one person in my life who always looks out for me.

I vividly remember another time when I escaped from my yard and went to visit her. It was 3:00 a.m. and her dogs were inside the house, barking, to let her know I was out there. She came outside to greet me and remembered I was the same dog that Celine and Sam returned. But this time my blue collar had a tag and phone number. Jolie called my owners and let me stay in her house until they came to get me. Twenty minutes later, she had to call a second time. Then Trish arrived apologetically and took me with her.

From that night on, I escaped repeatedly, and Jolie would find me in her driveway or somewhere on the block. I'm not exactly "street smart" and I could easily have been hit by a car. She must have gotten my back at least a dozen times.

19

Tad, one of the overnight sitters, springs through the front door all excited.

"Hannah, I think I found a home for Basil," he exclaims. "My next-door neighbor is an elderly lady who lives all alone. She always comments on how sweet my dog is. So lately we've been talking about her getting a dog for companionship. Since Basil is so laid back, I was thinking that it might be a perfect fit."

"Wow. That's great, Tad. Have her give me a call and we can set up a meet and greet."

"Sure thing. I'll call Mrs. Creighton right now."

Not much later, the front bells jingle jangle and she's here to meet me. I sniff her out. She doesn't seem to have much confidence. My gut is telling me this is a bad idea, but if Hannah and Tad think it's a good fit, then I trust them. I might just be feeling a little out of sync because Jolie isn't around.

After some chitchat, Hannah asks, "Mrs. Creighton, have you ever owned a dog before?"

"Why, yes. I used to have a wonderful golden retriever named Gus. It's been such a long time since he passed. I've always wanted another dog but just never got around to doing anything about it until Tad suggested I meet Basil."

Hearing her say that she's owned a dog before makes me feel a little better about her.

"Tad has offered to bring Basil to his house for play dates with his dog. I think that would be really good for Basil to have a friend right next door."

"I agree," says Hannah. "Mrs. Creighton, would you like to take Basil home for the night to see how it goes? I normally make a home visit, but Tad recommends you highly."

"Why, yes. I do believe I'm ready," says Mrs. Creighton.

Hannah takes a brand-new harness from its package and fits it to me before hooking on my leash.

"Mrs. Creighton, I'm sending you home with a harness that I want you to use every time you take Basil for a walk. That way you have more control over him than if you were to just use a leash. Watch how I attach it to Basil."

Mrs. Creighton watches Hannah. I, of course, stand there like a good boy.

"Now, let's have you take the harness off and put it back on, so you'll remember how to use it when you're at home."

Mrs. Creighton gets it wrong the first time, and Hannah gently corrects her. Again, I sense Mrs. Creighton's lack of confidence, but this time she gets it right and I'm ready for a walk.

The three of us walk out the front door and take a stroll up and down the street in front of Hannah's Haven. Hannah tells her, "It's important to remember that you're in control. Basil is as sweet as can be but he's still a dog and dogs can get excited when they see another dog, or when they see a cat, or a squirrel. But if you stay aware of your surroundings at all times, you can avoid most problems."

Mrs. Creighton says, "Tad tells me how gentle Basil is and that's what made me want to meet him. I can see that Tad is right."

After a short walk, we circle back. Knowing that I'll be leaving makes me sad and Hannah notices it by how my head is hanging a little lower than normal.

"Aw, Basil. It's all right. Mrs. Creighton is going

to take good care of you. You are going to be loved even more than you can imagine."

She's right. I can't imagine being loved more than Jolie loves me. And I don't even get to say goodbye.

20

Hannah walks out to Mrs. Creighton's car with us. I jump into the back seat and wait patiently while they say their goodbyes. Hannah reminds Mrs. Creighton, "If you have any questions or concerns, please reach out to me. And remember, if for any reason it doesn't work out, I promise to take Basil back."

Mrs. Creighton answers, "Oh, I'm sure we'll be just fine."

As Mrs. Creighton drives us to her house, I poke my nose out the window that she's lowered a few inches. There are so many scents that it's almost overwhelming. I just love being able to sniff the fresh air as we pass by people, cars, buses, restaurants, and even squirrels!

We arrive at my new home. Mrs. Creighton unhooks my leash and harness once we're in the house. I look around and like everything about it so far. Mrs. Creighton places a small, folded blanket on the floor in the living room. It's right next to her reclining chair. I assume that's where she wants me to lie down. She sits in her chair and puts the news on TV.

There's a knock on the front door. It's Tad!

"Hi, Mrs. Creighton. I told you I would give you my extra dog bowl and some food to get you through until you can get to the pet store. So here it is."

Tad kneels down to rub my back. It's sure nice to be around someone familiar.

"Well, Tad, that's awfully sweet of you. I really appreciate it. I'll make a trip to the pet store tomorrow and I'll return your bowl by tomorrow night."

"No worries, Mrs. Creighton. Take as long as you need. How's it going?"

"So far, so good. We're just relaxing. Basil's keeping me company while I watch the evening news."

"I just know you're going to love him. He's one of the sweetest and best-behaved dogs I've ever met. And it will be good for Winston to have a playmate. We'll give Basil a few days before we bring him over to my yard. That way it won't be too stressful for him. Besides, he needs to get used to his new surroundings."

"Well, Tad, I sure appreciate all you've done to help me."

"Sure thing, Mrs. Creighton. Just call if you need anything else."

Tad heads out the front door, closing it behind him.

Mrs. Creighton says to me, "Gee, Basil. It's already time for your walk. I think we should get a move on before it gets dark outside."

Mrs. Creighton fumbles with my harness. She can't remember which section goes over my head and which strap fastens under my belly. I wish I could show her. In her frustration, she gives up. Instead, she attaches the leash to my collar.

21

I'm a little nervous that Mrs. Creighton didn't follow Hannah's instructions, but I tell myself that everything will be okay. I'm not as excitable as some of the dogs I know, like the dogs who jump up on their humans when they see a leash, or the ones who run around in a circle so fast that their owners can't even clip the leash onto the collar.

Mrs. Creighton asks, "Are you ready, Basil?" I perk up my ears and look her in the eyes as a sign that I'm ready to go for a walk.

"Since this is our first walk, we're just going up and down the street. Tomorrow morning I'll take you around the whole block." She unlocks the front door and we step out onto the porch. She turns and shuts the door, locks it, then drops the key in her dress pocket.

I don't have a lot of experience walking on a leash, so I do my best to figure out how fast or slow I need to go to accommodate her. I don't think I'm going very fast but, all of a sudden, I feel a jerk on the leash, enough to stop me in my tracks. I turn around. Mrs. Creighton is on the ground. She looks pretty upset. I don't know what to do.

"Oh my goodness. I'm hurt! Basil, you're a bad dog!"

I hang my head. What did I do?

Mrs. Creighton yells, "Help! Please, someone help me!"

Luckily, Tad hears her and comes running toward us.

"Mrs. Creighton! I looked out my front window and saw you fall down. Are you okay? What happened? Here, let me help you up."

"Look! My knee is bleeding. Oh, and I've scraped my wrist too. He was walking so very fast that I couldn't keep up. I'm afraid this just isn't the dog for me."

"Here. Give me the leash. Now hold onto my arm and let me help you up. We'll get you back home and

I'll take care of your knee and your wrist. Do you hurt anywhere else?"

"No. I think I'm really just scared more than anything else. I'm so grateful you came to help me."

"I'm glad I was nearby. Okay. Let's take it slowly and get you inside."

The three of us walk back into her house. I avoid eye contact with Mrs. Creighton. With my head hung low and my tail tucked between my legs, I walk over to the blanket and curl up. My instincts were right. This isn't going to be my forever home.

Tad cleans up her scrapes. Mrs. Creighton confesses, "I didn't use the harness like Hannah showed me, but what difference could it make?"

Tad listens patiently and reassures her that a harness will give her better control. "I don't want to discuss it anymore," Mrs. Creighton states firmly.

She's not willing to give me a second chance. They decide that I'll spend the night at Tad's and he'll bring me back to Hannah's Haven in the morning.

Part of me is very sad. The other part is relieved. A dog needs the right owner. The person I dream of wakes up every morning excited about having me in their life. They will love me and take care of me. And I promise to love them and take care of them too.

22

G ood to her word, Hannah takes me back, and she's happy to see me. I spent the whole night worried and feeling rejected, but Hannah's joy lifts my mood.

Tad explains, "Mrs. Creighton decided she was too old to have a large dog. She hadn't used the harness when she walked Basil. Basil didn't do anything wrong. He was as gentle and sweet as he always is. It's just too bad that it wasn't a better fit. I guess it was my fault. I'm the one who thought they would be perfect together."

"Now, Tad, don't go blaming yourself. I've been through enough of these situations to know that even under the best of circumstances, there still can be surprises. Sure, I'm disappointed for Basil, but I trust that the universe is working on something even better for him. You'll see."

"Thanks, Hannah. I hope you're right." Tad reaches down and rubs my ear.

I hope she's right too.

Hannah senses I could use some attention and she lets me hang out with her in the office. The door is closed, but I can still hear a parade of dogs showing up for day care. I wonder who's here?

Hannah calls Colin from her cell phone. "Hi, honey. Guess what? Tad just brought Basil back. I guess it's time for me to put that ad on Petfinder. Keep your fingers crossed that someone awesome is looking for a dog just like Basil. Well, not just like Basil, but Basil!"

23

It's July first. Hannah has been fostering me for ten weeks. I'm hoping my luck improves soon.

After Hannah posts the ad on Petfinder.com, a nice couple named Mason and Stella shows up to meet me. I learn a lot about them by listening through the door in Hannah's office as the three of them talk in the lobby.

They tell Hannah that Mason is currently undergoing treatment for cancer. Stella is a nurse.

Stella says, "We had a dog that was our treasured family pet for twelve years until it passed away about three months ago. Ever since then, Mason has been battling depression. He's in bed when I leave for work in the morning. And when I get home after a twelve-hour shift, he's still in bed. I saw the Petfinder ad, and

Mason and I talked about getting another dog. He agreed that he was ready to open his heart again. Since we live across the street from a large park, anytime our new dog needs to go for a walk, it will also get Mason out of the house."

Hannah replies, "Well, I had hoped you would have a fenced-in yard, but this sounds like it might be a good fit."

I can't believe my ears. This sounds too good to be true. How lucky I would be if I could be their dog. All I can think is, I hope they like me.

The door to the office opens and Hannah announces, "Basil, I have some people I'd like you to meet. Basil, this is Mason and Stella. Mason and Stella, meet Basil."

I wait ever so patiently as they walk all the way across the room and sit on the couch. After they sit down, I put my head on Mason's lap, staring up at him with my big brown eyes. Of course, his hand lands on my head!

"What a sweetie. He's so gentle," says Mason.

Stella adds, "And he's so well-behaved. He didn't even jump up. Is he always this calm?"

Hannah and the two of them talk about me a whole lot. Suddenly, I feel like a rock star!

Hannah shares my entire history: how I was

surrendered to Jolie, how I've been fostered by Hannah for almost three months, how Mrs. Creighton brought me back after less than twenty-four hours because she was intimidated by my size. Hannah assures them that I'm one of the best dogs she has had the pleasure to rescue. She also tells them how good I am with Ivy.

Mason and Stella have grandkids and they're excited to hear I'm good with children. That's a real plus to have on one's resumé!

Hannah says, "Basil's been in rescue mode for several months now. He needs a forever home more than ever. It can have a negative effect if it isn't a good fit and he's brought back again. I don't know if he can take the disappointment. So how about if we set up a good time for you both for a home visit? I'll bring Basil to your house so I can evaluate if it's a good fit. It's part of the normal adoption process I go through with potential new owners for every dog I rescue."

Everyone agrees it's a great idea. Even me!

24

———

Bright and early the next morning, Hannah calls out, "Come on, Basil. We're going to check out Mason and Stella's home." This time I can't contain myself. I jump up and slurp Hannah's face.

"Aw, Basil. I don't want us to get our hopes up too high and possibly get disappointed, but I do have a really good feeling about them. My instincts tell me they need you as much as you need them. What could be better, eh boy?" Hannah attaches my leash and off we go.

Mason and Stella live in a lovely sprawling brick ranch house. The front walkway is lined with perky blue and yellow pansies.

"Could this be my new home?"

Mason is in the living room looking out their big bay window when he sees us pull up in the driveway. He answers the door before Hannah even has a chance to ring the bell. "Welcome. Come on in. Hey there, Basil!"

Wow! The inside of their house smells sweet.

"What a lovely home you have," says Hannah. "How long have you lived here?"

"We've been in this house going on thirty years. We raised our daughter here. It's a wonderful neighborhood. And there's a beautiful park across the street that we've enjoyed," Mason replies.

Stella walks into the living room with a big smile on her face, holding a plate of freshly baked chocolate chip cookies. "Hi there! Welcome to our home.

Thanks so much for coming out. Can I offer you a cookie?"

"Hi, Stella. It's good to see you again. I was just telling Mason that you have a lovely home. Why, yes, I'd love a cookie. Thank you," says Hannah.

Mason asks, "Would you like a tour? It's not real big, but it holds a lot of love. And we hope you think it's suitable for Basil."

Hannah and I walk through all the rooms as the three of them chat. In each room, I imagine myself living with them, where I will be fed, where we will all watch TV together.

When we get to their bedroom, Mason says, "Our last dog slept on the bed with us. We would, of course, let Basil sleep with us if he wants to."

Oh my gosh! Seriously? I hear this and jump up on the bed just to make sure they know I approve! Everyone laughs.

"As we mentioned, we don't have a fenced yard, but I can give Basil long walks in the park. Would you like to see it?"

"Sure," Hannah replies. She hands Mason my leash and off we go.

I've heard about dogs that assist humans. They are very special. They're called service dogs and they even wear special clothing. Right then and there I decide I'm going to assist Mason. I'll be his own personal angel and assist him any way I can for as long as I live. This feels so right.

Returning from our walk, Hannah says, "It looks like the three of you would be a great fit. That makes me really happy. How about if I leave the adoption forms with you and you bring them to me tomorrow at work? I usually charge a one hundred dollar adoption fee when I place a rescue, in order to cover my expenses. I took care of Basil for almost three months before you answered my ad, but since you're dealing with cancer, Mason, I'm happy to forgo the adoption fee. Think of Basil as my gift to you."

"Oh, Hannah, we are so thrilled. We will take excellent care of Basil. Thank you, thank you," says Mason.

"I know you will. Why don't you go ahead and make an appointment with your vet? That way you can bring me the forms, pick up Basil, and go straight to your vet for an initial intake appointment. Just give me a call when you're on your way. You know what? I just realized that you've been living without a dog for three months and that's how long Basil's been without a home. I think this was meant to be!"

This is so great. Tomorrow I am officially going to be a member of Team Mason!

25

I wake up with so much excitement in my body that I feel like dancing.

Jolie arrives and gives me a super huge hug. "Oh, Basil! I'm so happy to see you." She lovingly puts her hands on my face, then looks into my eyes and says, "I was so worried that you wouldn't be here when I got back from vacation. I guess that's a mixed blessing because we really need to find you a forever home, don't we?"

Leigh Ann appears, still in her pajamas. "Hey, Jolie. Welcome back. How was your vacation?"

"It was wonderful. I got to spend a lot of time with my family. I have to admit, though, I had Basil on my mind the whole time I was gone. I guess I'm more attached to him than I realized. How are things here?" she asks.

Leigh Ann tells Jolie, "Hannah finally placed an ad to find Basil a good home and then she took Basil for a home visit and everything went great and he's going to his new home today."

Hannah steps out of her office, her face creased in pain. "Something terrible happened."

"What?" Leigh Ann and Jolie ask in unison.

"You know Trish and Marina who used to own Basil? Trish saw the ad for Basil on Petfinder and she called me, crying. Trish and Victor are back together, and she and Marina moved back into Victor's house. Marina has been unbelievably distraught ever since she found out about her mother surrendering Basil. Marina cries herself to sleep every night, and insists she can't live without him. Trish even offered me money for him."

"You didn't . . ." Leigh Ann starts.

Hannah shakes her head. "Trish kept begging me, saying what a special dog Basil is, and how she should never have let Jolie take him."

"What?!!" Jolie says angrily. "Trish was going to take Basil to the Humane Association because he kept escaping. I only offered to find him a good home because she was so desperate and Victor insisted. So what did you say?"

"What could I say? I told her I was very sorry, but Basil had already been adopted."

"Wow! Thanks, Hannah. I'm glad you found him the perfect home. He's gonna have the life he deserves."

Tears well up in Jolie's eyes. "Did you hear that, Basil? Today's your adoption day. I guess these tears mean I'm having a gratitude attack. I feel so sad that you're leaving, buddy, but I'm also happy just knowing you're going to live happily ever after!"

Emotions can be complicated, especially when you feel two different ways. I'm going to miss Jolie too.

26

A s he promised Hannah, Mason does what every responsible pet owner does. He takes me to the vet for an exam. It includes some routine vaccines and lab tests.

Some dogs become afraid the moment they walk into a veterinary office, but not me. I think veterinarians are some of the most special people in the world. They know so much and only want the best for us critters. And unlike when a human goes to a doctor and explains what ails them, veterinarians have to piece together the clues our humans tell them about us in order to help us heal. Sometimes that includes needles and uncomfortable tests.

The vet tech enters the examination room with shots and an empty vial. A small portion of the fur on my front leg is shaved and they withdraw some of my blood. Not very much, just enough to fill the small vial. I don't even whimper. The vet tech scratches my head, saying, "You're a very good dog," and then she leaves the room.

I behave like a champ, making Mason proud of me.

Mason's first dog had been Dr. Friedman's patient. They chitchat about stuff: how Mason and Stella are doing, the crazy weather we've been having, and who the Titans are going to get to replace their running back, whatever that means. I don't mind hanging out in the exam room because, after all, I'm by Mason's side. He lovingly pets me the whole time they talk.

Dr. Friedman leaves the room to see if my test results are ready. He steps back in a few moments later, holding a piece of paper that he places in my chart.

"Basil seems like a relatively healthy dog, except his test for heartworms came out positive. Unfortunately, we don't know how long he's had them, but since he's young, the prognosis is good."

Mason has a concerned look on his face. "Heartworms?"

Dr. Friedman explains, "Heartworms are worms

that live in a dog's heart. They are transmitted by mosquitoes. If a mosquito that's transmitting heartworms bites a dog, it leaves heartworm larvae that quickly enters into the hole the mosquito made. It then begins to mature in the dog's body. After going through several different phases, it ultimately gets into the animal's circulation and goes to the heart, where they do their final maturation. As heartworms develop, the heart reacts and becomes less efficient.

"If we have a young patient with a high worm load that's not had the problem for very long, we do the treatment in one fell swoop: two shots given twenty-four hours apart.

"If they're sicker, older, or have other problems where they might be more severely compromised by the whole scope of treatment, then we can separate the treatment and do one shot, get a partial kill on the heartworms — some will live, some will die — and then come back in a month and do the two shots."

All three of us listen intently.

"Part of the complication of heartworm treatment is that these worms don't just vanish. The good news is, if we do the two-stage treatment of one shot and then two shots, there aren't as many worms arriving in the lung tissue. The body can probably get rid of them a little bit more safely and efficiently."

Mason and Stella each breathe a sigh of relief.

Dr. Friedman continues, "I'm guessing that Basil is around three to four years old, so in his case, not knowing how long he's had heartworms, I highly recommend the two-stage treatment of one shot and then two shots."

Mason and Stella look at each other, and then Mason looks back at Dr. Friedman. "I think Stella and I should go home and talk about it. Can we get back to you?"

"Of course. I wouldn't wait too long, but I'm sure a few days or so won't make too much of a difference."

On the drive home, Mason keeps the car window down. I catch the wind in my cheeks.

27

We return home and Mason calls Hannah. As the two of us sit on the couch in the sunroom, Mason gently strokes my head while he shares the gloomy news.

"Hi, Hannah. It's Mason. Is this a good time to talk?"

"Sure, Mason. You sound a little down. Is something wrong?"

"Well, yes. We took Basil to our vet this morning and discovered that he has heartworms. Our vet said it's treatable but it's a lot for Basil to go through until he's back in good health. I thought you'd like to know. It's really taken us by surprise."

"Gee. I'm so sorry to hear this. Believe it or not, I've never had to deal with heartworms before. I hear the medicine is pretty hard on a dog's system, not to mention how expensive it is. A good friend of mine knows all about holistic medicine. How about if I reach out to her to see what would be involved to treat Basil holistically? I'm sure it would cost way less than conventional treatment. I'll do some research on my end and will call you back in a couple of days. How does that sound? Are you still interested in keeping Basil, because I will gladly take him back if you feel this is more than you want to deal with."

"No worries. He's a member of our family now. We just weren't expecting this, especially since the treatment could cost over five hundred dollars."

"I understand. Let me see what I can find out and I'll give you a call once I know more. I'm pretty sure that treating him holistically will cost less."

"Okay. Thanks, Hannah. We look forward to hearing from you."

Mason puts down his phone and looks directly into my eyes. "Basil, I know how it feels to be sick. Your health is super important to us and we'll do whatever it takes to help you get well. You can count on that."

He leans over, wraps his arms around me, and gives me a long hug. Is that a tear I feel?

28

J olie is working the front desk and overhears bits and pieces of Hannah and Mason's conversation. Jolie asks, "Is Mason calling with bad news?"

"I'm afraid so," says Hannah. "Apparently, Basil has heartworms. It's never good when a dog has heartworms and it really frustrates me because they're preventable with a monthly pill."

"Poor guy. I'm not surprised that he has them, considering the way his previous owners treated him."

"I know," replies Hannah. "I told Mason I'd do some research about treating heartworms with holistic medicine. It's a lot less taxing on a dog's body. I know some people I can call who have used it."

"Hannah, would you mind if I call Mason? I'd like him to know how much I care so he feels supported."

"Sure. No problem. I'll text you his number."

That night when Jolie and her husband, Harlan, sit down to dinner, she tells him the bad news about Basil.

"I've been so upset all day. The worst part is that Hannah suggested treating Basil through holistic medicine. I'm a big believer in treating certain things holistically, but I don't like the idea of using it as the only protocol to treat something as dangerous as heartworms. Homeopathy is a great way to support the immune system alongside conventional treatment. I really do believe that veterinary medicine is the safest way to treat something as serious as this."

"Have you talked to Mason?" asks Harlan.

"No. Not yet. I'm too upset so I thought I'd call him tomorrow when I'm less freaked out," Jolie replies.

"I've got a great idea! You know how I've been saving all the washers and dryers and refrigerators from when we make upgrades in our rental proper-ties? I have a whole garage full that we can clean up and sell on Craigslist. We can earmark every penny to go towards Basil's treatment. I'm sure we can easily raise at least $400, maybe $500. Then it won't be such a financial burden on Mason and Stella. Plus, if Basil goes to our vet, he'll be given the best possible care and it won't cost as much as other veterinarians. What do you think?"

"Wow! That's so brilliant! I bet Mason will go for it. Why wouldn't he?"

Harlan adds, "Why don't you call Mason after dinner? I'm sure he'd love to hear some good news."

"I will!"

Later that night, after Mason and Jolie speak, he shares his excitement with Stella.

"That was Jolie. She wanted to tell me her thoughts on the importance of having Basil treated by a vet instead of only with homeopathic remedies because of the seriousness of his condition. Everything she said makes sense, and now that I understand it better, I agree."

Mason continues talking to Stella, tears welling up in his eyes. His voice is choked up. "Jolie and her husband have offered to pay for the full treatment if we'll take Basil to their vet. They've been clients there for over twenty years and they completely trust their vet's judgment. Admittedly, it's a longer drive for us, but I feel confident that Basil will be in good hands. I'm so touched by their generous offer. What do you think?"

Getting up from her favorite overstuffed chair, Stella gives Mason a big hug. "Sweetheart, don't you worry. We will do whatever it takes to get Basil healthy."

Then I get a hug from Stella too!

29

The very first thing the next morning, Mason calls Dr. Triggs at Grass Valley Animal Hospital. After finishing his phone consultation, Mason explains everything to Stella.

"That was a long conversation. What did she say? Is everything okay?" asks Stella.

"Yes. I believe it's all going to be okay," replies Mason. "Dr. Triggs agreed with Dr. Friedman's recommendation of doing the two-stage treatment. She explained that before we can begin the actual treatment, Basil needs to be on antibiotics for a month. Apparently, there's a little germ that lives inside the heartworms. The antibiotic will kill it and by doing that, it weakens the heartworms so then the heartworm treatment can work even better because the germ inside the worm is dead."

Since Stella is a nurse, she quickly understands. Nodding, she says, "Go on."

"After Basil finishes taking the antibiotic for thirty days, we'll bring him in for his first shot. We'll need to keep Basil calm to prevent a big wad of half-dead worms from breaking off and entering his circulation. If a big clump of heartworms did lodge in an artery or vein somewhere, it could cut off his circulation. And the most common place they would do that —" Mason pauses and takes a deep breath before continuing — "would be his lungs. Dr. Triggs said the only times they've really had any problem is when dog owners don't restrict their dog's activity."

"We'll make sure we do exactly what Dr. Triggs tells us," says Stella.

"The good news is that he doesn't have to be boarded and he'll be treated entirely as an outpatient. He doesn't ever have to spend one night away from us.

"Dr. Triggs says they like to see the dogs they've treated again around three months after the initial treatment. She'll listen to Basil's heart and lungs, check his weight and make sure he's doing okay.

"And by giving Basil heartworm prevention

tablets every month, we'll be protecting him because it kills any baby heartworms.

"I'll meet Dr. Triggs when I pick up the antibiotic."

Then, while looking at me, Mason says, "We're in this together, pal. And you're getting the best care possible. All you have to do is stay calm and we'll do the rest."

My wagging tail gives Mason and Stella a sign that I understand. I feel the love in the room.

F or Sale: Whirlpool full-size matching washer &
dryer, five years old, excellent condition $300
for the pair. Apartment-size portable dishwasher -
works great $75. Kenmore white refrigerator, a few
scratches on the side, perfect for a small space, runs
well $100. Located in East Nashville. All proceeds
from the sale of these items are going toward medical
treatment for a dog we rescued. If interested, please
respond by email and include your phone number. We
will respond to all messages promptly.

That's how the Craigslist ad read. In only one day,
Harlan and Jolie raised enough money for my treatment. And not even one person asked if they would
come down in price, because they knew their money
was going toward a good cause. ME!

I've been on the antibiotic for a month and today is the day I go for my first heartworm treatment. I wake up feeling happy. I'm happy that I'm able to go to a veterinarian who's helping me get well. I'm happy because this isn't going to be a financial struggle for Mason and Stella and I'm happy because I used to only dream of belonging to a family, and now I have one of my very own.

The drive to Dr. Triggs's office seems to go on forever. I've never been in a car for so long. Mason and Stella ride in the front seat and I ride in the back. The seat belt is threaded through my leash, to keep me from bouncing around.

I sense Mason and Stella are feeling stressed. Feeling what my humans are feeling is one of my superpowers. A lot of dogs have that superpower. If I could, I'd tell them, "No need to worry. We're going to get through this just fine." But then I start second-guessing myself and wonder if they know more than me about my condition. Maybe I should be worried. But then I remember the helpful little tune Jolie sang to me. "Hey. You're okay. You'll be fine. Just breathe."

We arrive at the animal hospital and are greeted by a very kind lady at the front desk. Her name is Zina and it's obvious that she loves animals very much.

The main waiting area is for dogs. They have a smaller section reserved for cats. Of course, it gets my curiosity up because of all the scents that are coming from that area. But I'm not allowed to even peek behind the partition to the section reserved for cats and kittens.

Zina gathers the paperwork that the other clinic sent over and Mason signs some papers.

Zina says, "A vet tech will come get Basil in just a moment."

I think back to the time I spent at Hannah's Haven and how, when nervous dogs arrived, they were put in a special area with just me. I was always the calm and confident dog. Today is no different. I assure Mason and Stella that I'm not afraid. I keep my tail high and lick Mason's face as he bends down and hugs me tight. "Oh, Basil. I just love you so much."

The vet tech appears. Mason hands her my leash and I follow her lead into the back room while my family waits for me.

This hospital for animals is a really cool place. I say that because everyone here loves helping animals, and that love shows in the way they treat me. They help me get up onto a big metal table. It's covered with a soft towel so it isn't too cold. Once I'm up there, I have to stay still or I will fall off. Maybe that's why they put me on the table. If I were on the floor, there's a lot more room to squirm and explore the scents left behind from other animals.

Dr. Triggs comes in with my chart in her hands. Her calm and confident vibe makes me trust her instantly as she rubs my ear and looks into my eyes. Her voice is soothing.

After listening to my heart with her stethoscope, she tells me, "Okay, Basil. We're just going to give you a shot and then you get to go home."

The vet tech hands her a syringe and a vial of medicine. Dr. Triggs is really good at giving shots and it's over in a snap. "There you go, buddy. All done. We'll see you back here in a month."

*"Dr. Triggs listens to my heart with her
stethoscope."*

Dr. Triggs lowers me off the table and walks me back through the door to the waiting room. Look, Mason and Stella. I'm all done! They both smile when they see me.

During the ride home, they tune into a music station with soothing music and no words because they think it will help me stay relaxed. I think it helps Mason and Stella relax.

32

My second heartworm treatment was exactly like the first. It consisted of a shot in my back, only this time they gave it to me on the opposite side of my spine. I was sore where Dr. Triggs gave me the injection. I still have to remain calm. No jumping on the couch and no rolling around in autumn leaves to hear them crackle and crunch.

We pull into our driveway and Mason says, "I'm going to take Basil for a short walk in the park."

"I think that's a great idea. Nothing strenuous should be fine."

"Okay. We'll be back in a bit."

Mason picks out a bench where there aren't many dogs or people passing by. I climb up and sit next to him. We sit in silence for a while. Mason is deep in thought.

"Basil, what would I do without you? I feel so isolated lately. I don't want Stella to see how tired the chemo makes me. I know it will pass. No sense in worrying her, right? I feel safe with you by my side. And I can confide in you. I love you so much." Mason takes a deep breath and exhales slowly. He wipes a tear from his eye. "Come on, buddy. Let's get you home."

We walk back into the house. Mason greets Stella with a kiss.

"I think Basil could use a nap. Getting that shot was pretty stressful for him. We're going to go lie down."

"All right, sweetheart. Enjoy your nap."

I wish I could tell Mason how much I love him too.

33

I t's the day after my second shot and I go back to Grass Valley for the third and final dose.

Dr. Triggs tells Mason and Stella, "These last thirty days are extremely important to the success of Basil's treatment. As I mentioned before, the only real time we have any complications from this treatment is when dog owners do not restrict activity.

"I'm sending Basil home with a broad-spectrum antibiotic. I'd like you to start giving it to him a week from today, and I'm giving you enough for ten days. This is an extra measure we like to take to keep Basil from getting pneumonia while the worms are breaking down. I'm also sending you home with heartworm prevention medicine that you can start giving Basil once a month for the rest of his life.

You'll start this in thirty days. And lastly, I'd like to take a look at Basil in two months' time. Of course, you don't have to wait until then to call me if you have any questions. I'm here to help."

"Thank you so much, Dr. Triggs. We are so grateful for your kindness and your expertise."

"And you have such a wonderful staff here," adds Stella.

"It's been my pleasure. And I understand that my services and all the medicine have been covered by someone who also loves Basil very much! You take care and don't hesitate to call me if you have any questions."

"Will do," replies Mason.

"Goodbye y'all," says Zina, as we walk out the front door.

I think back to the day my life first took a turn for the better, the day last May that Jolie rescued me during that scary storm, the day that Trish surrendered me to her. And I think of all the crazy things that had to happen in order to bring me to this exact moment in time.

34

It's been three months since I had my first heartworm shot. The journey hasn't been easy, but it's been worth it. There were some days when my back hurt so much that I didn't even want to get up to eat, but I did, in spite of how I felt. I never want to give Mason a reason to worry.

I'm feeling so much better than when I started treatment last August. I'm happy to be alive. Mason is the owner I've always dreamed of. He gently strokes my back or rubs my belly, and even though I weigh about sixty pounds, he lets me climb up on his lap. My water bowl is always full of fresh water. I never have to worry about any other dog stealing my food. And Mason and Stella actually want me to sleep on the bed with them. I really hit the doggie jackpot!

It's time to see Dr. Triggs for our final visit. Mason hooks my leash to my collar and walks me out to the car while Stella locks the front door.

When we arrive at Grass Valley Animal Hospital, Zina greets us all with a big smile. "Hey y'all. How's Basil doin'?"

"Great," Mason responds. "Aren't you, Basil?"

I wag my tail and try to get Mason to move closer to the area that's just for cats, but he realizes what I'm up to and walks me over to a row of chairs at the far end of the room where we all sit and wait.

Dr. Triggs opens the door to the waiting room. "Hey there, Basil. It's your turn."

Dr. Triggs gives me a thorough examination. She listens to my heart and lungs through her stethoscope, then feels my belly. "Have you started Basil on the heartworm preventative?"

Mason answers, "Yes. We marked it on our calendar so we won't miss a monthly dose."

"Great. I'd say that Basil should have a long and healthy life ahead of him. He's lucky to have such a wonderful home."

"Oh, we're the lucky ones," says Mason.

"I'll say," adds Stella. "Our grandkids just adore him!"

"That's how it should be. Okay, Basil. You take

care, buddy." Dr. Triggs walks us out and hands my file to Zina to check us out.

We head home and again I get to ride with my head out the window, so happy to feel the breeze on my face!

". . . so happy to feel the breeze on my face!"

35

Today is my first Thanksgiving celebration with Mason and Stella. Actually, it's my first Thanksgiving ever. The dining room table is set with a beautiful white linen tablecloth that apparently Stella only uses for special occasions. Places are set for Mason and Stella, and their daughter, Brooklyn, and her husband, Nikhil, and their two children, Amita and Ashok.

It's almost dinnertime and Brooklyn walks through the front door carrying food that smells absolutely delicious! The rest of the family follows her. Nikhil is also carrying a platter of food in his arms, and the aroma is fantastic! I forget my manners and jump up to get a closer whiff.

"Whoa! Down, Basil!" says Mason.

Oops! I didn't mean to upset him!

"Hi, Mom and Dad."

Amita and Ashok come running in. They throw their arms around Stella, each giving her a big hug.

"Oh, you two! You give the best hugs," says Stella.

"Happy Thanksgiving, Grandma," Amita and Ashok tell her in unison. Amita and Ashok then throw their arms around Mason and hug him.

Then the kids give me kisses and hugs. Amita loves to smooch me all over my head. She says things like, "Oh, Basil, you are so pretty," and "How's my Basil-bell today?"

The kids turn to Mason, "Grandpa, can we take Basil for a walk? Please? Please?"

Mason smiles. "Of course. Let me get his leash and we'll head out to the park."

As we leave the house, Stella calls out, "Don't be too long. Dinner will be ready soon."

Amita and Ashok both want to hold my leash, but Mason reminds them that walking by his side makes me feel safe, so for now, he will do the leash-holding. They hold hands as we take our time crossing the street, looking both ways before stepping off the curb. Mason's correct. I do feel safe by his side.

The park is pretty empty since it's a holiday and

most people are home. It's cold out, with a fall crispness in the air, but the sun is shining and it feels good to me. The kids love to skip on the dirt path through the park. Mason reminds them not to get too far ahead of us.

We reach the playground area and the kids each sit on a swing. Mason and I find a nearby bench and sit and watch as they kick their feet forward, then pull them back, increasing how high they can go. Mason reaches over and scratches under my collar.

After a while, Mason calls to them, "C'mon, you two! I think it's about time to head back." Amita and Ashok are two little bundles of energy, skipping all the way back across the park. Again, everyone holds hands. We look both ways and cross the street. The kids go running up to the house. "That was so much fun, Grandpa. Thanks!"

Mason opens the front door and unhooks my leash. Brooklyn greets us and says, "Okay, kids. Let's wash our hands. Dinner is ready!"

Mason is a little tired from our walk but I'm the only one who notices. As he takes his place at the head of the table, I take my place on the floor by his side. The rest of the family joins us.

"Okay, everyone! Let's start with our Thanksgiving tradition," says Stella. "I'm grateful to have all of our family together in our home to celebrate this day."

Brooklyn says, "I'm grateful that I have such an awesome family."

Nikhil adds, "I'm very grateful that I found a new job this year and I'm able to provide for my family."

Amita says, "I'm grateful for all my friends and all the new toys I got for my birthday."

"I have a birthday soon!" adds Ashok.

Stella chimes in, "Yes, you do. And can you tell us one thing you're feeling grateful for today?"

Ashok says, "I know. I'm grateful that we get to eat Grandma's yummy cooking."

Everyone laughs.

Mason takes a moment to hold back his tears. "I'm grateful that we were able to welcome Basil into our family this year because he helped fill the empty place in my heart after Skipper died, and he gives me a special reason to get out of bed every single day."

And I am grateful for each and every rescuer who helped me on my quest for a good life. I will always carry them with me in my heart. But the most special place in my heart is for my furever family, who healed my broken heart and made my dream come true.

ACKNOWLEDGMENTS

And the day came when the risk to remain tight in a bud was more painful than the risk it took to blossom. – Anaïs Nin

Writing *Basil's Quest, A Tale of Dogged Determination,* was not a single-handed accomplishment. The universe sent me helpers. Each of their unique threads were woven into the beautiful tapestry of the story you hold in your hands. They helped me take a risk and encouraged me to blossom.

To my amazing family: I love you so much! Thank you for loving me, for always supporting my creative endeavors, and for being my constant cheerleaders! I hit the trifecta!

To my editor, Tina Levine: How lucky I am to have you as my friend and now my editor. Thank you for making me a better writer.

To Amanda Penecale: Thank you for capturing Basil's joyful spirit with your beautiful illustrations.

To Carol L. Macherey, DVM, and Walter Clark, DVM, DABVP, of Grassmere Animal Hospital: Thank you for generously spending time with me explaining the intricacies of heartworms.

To Ze Frank: Thank you for permission to use lyrics from your Chillout song. I'm so glad I stumbled onto your TED Talk.

To Mark Bryan: Thank you for giving this single mom a spot in your Artist's Way workshop in 1995. Your kindness and generosity ignited the spark that led me to live a more creative and fulfilling life.

To my Kickstarter backers: Thank you for your generous support and for believing in this project.

To Katie McDougall: Thank you for your insightful teaching and gentle guidance during your Draft First Aid Workshop at The Porch. And thanks to workshop attendees who provided most excellent feedback in a way that I could hear it.

To my young beta readers: Lilly Bergman, Alex Cavolo, CJ Cavolo, and Emily Dunn. Thank you! You helped me more than you know.

To my adult beta readers: Hosana Banks, Sonia Cavolo, Elizabeth Chauncey, Martha Geel, Zina Goodin, Vickie Harris, Kelly Jennings, Susan Kelley, and Tara Rose: Thank you for your willingness to spend time with Basil, and for your invaluable feedback.

To Heidi Dixner of Red Rover Pet Services, Darlene Jacobs and Ann Anderson of Peace Love and Paws, Elizabeth Chauncey of East C.A.N., and Vickie Harris of Music City Animal Rescue: You inspire me with your selflessness and love for animals.

And to all those who generously give their time and energy to rescue, foster, rehabilitate, nurture, adopt, transport, and find loving forever homes for animals like Basil - - you rock!

ABOUT THE AUTHOR

Gracie H. Vandiver

Gracie Vandiver has rescued many animals, but one dog rescue in particular stood out enough to write a book based on her experience. *Basil's Quest, A Tale of Dogged Determination,* is Gracie Vandiver's first adventure in children's book writing. She shares her love of books as the steward of her Little Free Library (charter #83579 located in Nashville, Tennessee), providing free access to books through neighborhood bookcases maintained by volunteers. Gracie and her husband, Jerry, are active in the rescue dog transporting community, helping homeless animals relocate to states where they have a better chance of being adopted.

Learn more about Gracie at gracievandiver.com.

CPSIA information can be obtained
at www.ICGtesting.com
Printed in the USA
LVHW080944120921
697403LV00004BA/12